JAMES COOK

A Life From Beginning to End

Copyright © 2017 by Hourly History.

Table of Contents

Introduction

Before the famous voyages of Captain James Cook, the Atlantic Ocean was the main arena for European voyages of discovery. While England did engage in exploration, it was simply not in the same league as countries like Spain, Portugal, and France. English expeditions were neither as ambitious or successful as those of several continental nations.

No European country, whether British or continental, had yet accurately mapped the Pacific Ocean. There was no inkling that a place like Australia was out there, and the question of whether a great southern continent could exist was by no means answered.

Few would have suspected that James Cook was destined to change this when he was born to a poor family in Yorkshire. At that time, in the eighteenth century, Great Britain was a strictly stratified society. There was virtually no social mobility, and individuals from humble circumstances who managed to climb the social ladder were truly few and far between.

One of the small number of places in British society where someone like Cook had a hope of achieving a level of greatness was the Royal Navy. As a youth, it seemed that Cook would spend his life as a farm worker, like his father. A fateful move and an attraction to the sea, however, intervened and set the young man on a path to historic voyages and discoveries.

James Cook brought more of a scientific approach to exploration than had been used before. This methodology allowed the accomplishments that led to Cook's immortal fame. Cook is also remembered for the strictly disciplined routine he imposed on his ship crews to help ensure health and hygiene, as well as efficiency. Unfortunately, Cook took an overly forceful approach with the indigenous populations he encountered. There can be no doubt, however, about Cook's significance and his impact on history.

Chapter One

Cook's Early Days and Journey to North America

"Ambition leads me not only farther than any other man has been before me, but as far as I think it possible for man to go."

—James Cook

James Cook was born on October 27, 1728, in the small Yorkshire village of Marton near Middlesbrough. Cook's father, also called James, was an agricultural worker. The elder James Cook had moved to Yorkshire from Scotland after the Jacobite rebellion of 1715 and fell in love with a woman named Grace Pace, who was from Thornaby on Tees. Grace gave birth to the future Captain James Cook in a humble cottage made of stone with a thatch roof. The cottage is believed to have had only two rooms and possibly mud walls.

James and Grace Cook had eight children, but five of them appear to have died in childhood. The survivors were James and two sisters, Christiana and Margaret. Margaret, born in 1742, would eventually marry a man named James Fleck, while Christiana, born in 1731 or 1732, married a fisherman. Christiana lived until the mature age of 64 in 1795, while Margaret died at the age of 62 in 1804.

Because of James' father's work and the hope of a better place to live, the Cooks moved back and forth between Marton and closeby Ormesby a number of times. In around 1736, the elder James was promoted to the position of foreman at Aireyholme Farm. It is thought that the family then lived in one of that farm's estate cottages, and James received a basic education at the village school. After he had left school, he followed in his father's footsteps and obtained farm work.

James' mental energy and ambition, however, made farm work an unsuitable calling for him. He felt compelled to seek out better opportunities and arenas in which he could make better use of his mental facilities. His parents wanted him to have a more fulfilling life than they had been able to enjoy, and they did not object when James wanted to leave. In 1745, James moved to Staithes to work for a merchant, grocer, and haberdasher called William Sanderson. The Sanderson's shop was situated on the seafront of the fishing village, and it was there that Cook first saw and grew to love the sea.

Although Cook had been happy with his job at the grocer and haberdasher's at first, his ambitions made him eager to make a greater mark in the world than would be possible on his current trajectory. After spending less than one year at the shop, Cook made his wishes known to Sanderson. As Cook was an apprentice, Sanderson could have thwarted his dreams, at least for a significant amount of time. Luckily, however, Sanderson was good-natured enough not to try to stop Cook from following his dreams of a life at sea.

In 1746, Cook left Staithes to become an apprentice to a ship owner and coal merchant named John Walker. To his great excitement, Cook had the opportunity to sail on a number of vessels. During the winter months, he lived with the Walker family in Whitby along with other apprentices and spent his time studying. The Walkers were a strict Quaker family, and they instilled a sense of strong discipline into the young man. They also encouraged him in his dreams and made him realize that he had what it took to go further as a mariner.

In 1755, Cook decided on a career with the Royal Navy and set off to achieve his new calling. It may seem strange to us today, but at this time it was unusual for men to choose such an occupation. Because of the unpopularity of enlisting in the Navy, it had to force people in, through such methods as violently detaining men in harbors and even kidnapping individuals from commercial ships. Being in the Royal Navy, especially in a lowly position in the hierarchy, was a difficult life full of privation of various kinds. Men in the Navy were forced to be away from their families and friends for long stretches of time, and life onboard a ship was one of unremitting duty and routine.

Cook was not so easily deterred, and at the very beginning of his career in the Navy, he participated in the patrolling of Scottish waters, the Irish sea, the English Channel, and coastal areas of France. This was part of the effort to protect British territory, as the country was in conflict with France at the time.

The first ship on which James Cook sailed in the Royal Navy was *The Eagle*. It was commanded by Sir Hugh Palliser, who was soon impressed by Cook's enthusiasm and skill. Sir Hugh Palliser was born in 1722 in Yorkshire. His family was of the gentry, and they had a large estate at Newby Wiske. But being the younger son, Palliser had to find a profession where he could, because of the rules of primogeniture, in which the estate in its entirety must go to the eldest son. And so, he entered the Navy and became a captain of foot.

In 1758, James Cook left European waters and was sent to North America. People tend to forget that Cook would spend as many as nine years in Newfoundland, Quebec (then referred to as Lower Canada), and Nova Scotia. It was during these instrumental years he developed the knowledge and skills that would one day make him famous. The young man was a remarkably fast learner, and he became proficient in complex endeavors that most other men of the same age would have found overwhelming. During this period, Cook's official naval title or rank was that of master.

Like Cook, Sir Hugh Palliser had a genuine love of and enthusiasm for the sea, and he enjoyed the respect and appreciation of his superiors. Even though Palliser was from a well-established family, he still lacked the level of connections and patronage that some other young men possessed. Through hard work and determination (and the help of the patronage he did have), he established a successful career and rose through the ranks.

Palliser gave Cook the position of NCO, non-commissioned officer, two years later. Sir Hugh Palliser remained an important advocate for James Cook and his talents for a long time to follow. This endorsement, of which Cook must have been very proud, helped to make up for Cook's lack of social connections and the patronage in the Royal Navy that they could bring. While it would take him longer to progress through the power structure than others with much less natural talent, ability, and drive, the opportunity that Palliser gave him at least made it possible that he would one day be able to overcome the social obstacles he faced.

James Cook's first long voyage and opportunity to show his potential was on a ship called the *Mercury*, which was sailing to Canada to fight the French. Cook, appointed master of the ship, made the significant accomplishment of charting the St. Lawrence River. This feat brought him to the notice of people far up the Royal Navy chain, as it was Cook's map that permitted the British to make crucial impact in a decisive battle in Quebec. As a result, Cook was awarded the position of steersman. He was also made a navy surveillance assistant under the supervision of a Captain Grenville.

In 1759, Cook spent at least six months in the waters near New York and Boston. Cook was often called upon to act as a messenger during this general time period, bringing essential information to fellow British naval men to help them defeat the French in the conflict over territory in North America. Soon after this, Cook returned for a visit to England.

The following four years, from 1763 to 1767, Cook spent most of his time in waters near Newfoundland, Labrador, and Nova Scotia, as he was made responsible for surveying the waters near these territories. This was a significant assignment that would only rarely be assigned to someone as young and relatively inexperienced as Cook. To be trusted with such a task clearly demonstrated how respected Cook now was by his superiors.

The charting of Newfoundland's waters alone would take him several years, and it was on this coast that Cook first observed a solar eclipse. He made detailed records of the eclipse which were later published by the Royal Society of London, perhaps the longest established learned society in the world. The Royal Society is devoted to the scientific disciplines and discoveries that are made through experimental investigation; it was given its royal charter by King Charles in 1660. Cook would cooperate with the Royal Society many more times throughout his career.

In between Cook's years spent at sea, he managed to marry one of his mentor's daughters, Elizabeth Batts in December 1762, during one of his visits to England. The ceremony took place in Barking, Essex, to the east of London. Over the next thirteen years, James and Elizabeth had six children: James, born in 1763, Nathaniel, in 1764, Elizabeth, in 1767, Joseph, in 1768, George, in 1772, and finally Hugh Cook, born in 1776. Tragically, most of the children died when they were very young, a common occurrence in the eighteenth century. James and George died as infants, Elizabeth passed when she was four years old, Nathaniel when he was sixteen, and Hugh at seventeen.

Only one year after marrying Elizabeth, Cook set out on his journey to survey Newfoundland in 1763. This was a sign of what was to come. During his career, Cook would be away from Elizabeth and the children the majority of the time. The husband and wife were married for about seventeen years, but are estimated to have spent perhaps four of them in the same country.

Little is known about James Cook's personal life and relationship with his family, but there seems little reason to doubt that he loved his wife and children. Elizabeth burned the many letters that James had sent her over the years while he was at sea before she died at an old age. It appears likely that she did this to avoid personal information from being leaked to the press, as James Cook was by that time at the height of his fame as a national hero and there was a great deal of curiosity about him.

Chapter Two

Cook's First Great Voyage: The Endeavour (1768-1771)

"Do just once what others say you can't do, and you will never pay attention to their limitations again."

—James Cook

James Cook's first time leading a voyage began in 1768. His ship was called the H.M.S. *Endeavour*, and it set off from Plymouth in August of that year. The ostensible reason for the expedition was the Royal Society's wish that someone make detailed notes of observations concerning a rare astronomical event—the passing of Venus before the sun. The best place to observe this passing would be in the southern hemisphere. But the more important rationale for this adventure southward—and one that was not spoken of outside of official circles—was to find out if the fabled southern continent, now known as Antarctica, existed.

The class-based structure and intrinsic unfairness of British society at the time was reflected in the fact that although James Cook was the person who would be leading the expedition and had the skills needed to make it a success, a man called Joseph Banks was officially the person in charge. Banks was a naturalist from the landed gentry who had been educated at Oxford and had the connections and social clout that Cook lacked. Wealthy gentlemen like Banks were able to pay large sums of money that allowed them to take part in exciting expeditions.

Success in the Royal Navy depended a great deal on your connections in the naval structure of command, and how far those connections would go to advocate for your promotion. Without having been born in a genteel family or the connections that birth was likely to bestow, your skill and talent had to be of the highest caliber to have any hope of making meaningful progress through the power structure, and even if you managed it, it was likely to take a very long time.

James Cook, who was on that uphill struggle in the chain of command, was given the authority to choose the ship that would be used for the voyage. He selected a freight ship that had in earlier times been used to transport coal. His reasoning for this appears to have been that the vessel had a lot of cargo space, did not require a large crew, and would be able to approach coasts more closely than ships made for the military.

Cook ordered that the ship have supplies such as pickled carrots, sauerkraut, water, beer, and biscuits. Unlike many other people at the time, he understood the critical importance in vegetables to prevent scurvy in ship crews. Everyone on the vessel, including Joseph Banks and anyone who might have looked down on Cook socially, was fortunate that Cook was allowed this level of responsibility. The young man was gifted at understanding what was necessary for a safe and fruitful voyage, and the crew who sailed with him invariably benefited.

As this was officially a scientific journey, the ship was also stocked with equipment such as pots for plants, glass jars, paints and canvasses for drawing what was seen, and more writing materials than would typically be needed. There were also salts and waxes to preserve seeds from plants they might come upon, as well as alcohol specifically meant to be used in the preservation of newly discovered animals.

The *Endeavour* had its necessary upgrades completed by the end of July in 1768 when it first left Deptford Basin, after which it stopped at Gallions Reach to stock up on ammunition and guns. Three weeks later, it arrived in Portsmouth, and on August 26, 1768, the *Endeavour* officially began the voyage with 94 people aboard.

The crew had to sail through the Bay of Biscay, which is a gulf situated in the northeast Atlantic, touching both Spain and France. Around 86,000 square miles in size, the Bay of Biscay often experiences severe and dangerous storms. Making it through unscathed, the ship then passed along Portugal's coast and eventually made its way westward across the Atlantic. The crew then had to find the trade winds in order to sail the ship towards the equator. The trade winds came to have that name because they had been used for hundreds of years for the movement of goods by ship, first by the Portuguese. These winds could be experienced in the tropics and were surface winds easterly in direction. In the southern hemisphere, the winds blew mainly to the southeast, while the primary direction in the northern hemisphere was from the northeast.

During the long journey across the Atlantic, Cook was entertained by the opportunity of speaking in depth on topics that interested him with university-educated men, such as Joseph Banks and the other scientists and researchers who accompanied him.

Eventually, the ship reached and overcame the obstacle of Cape Horn in Chile, which is the point where the Atlantic and the Pacific meet. Cape Horn is located in Tierra del Fuego, an archipelago situated at South America's southernmost point. To successfully sail around Cape Horn was a major accomplishment for any ship and its officers and crew. The cape had many hazards, including icebergs, strong currents, and formidable winds and waves. Many ships were wrecked and sank there over the years.

Once the *Endeavour* had made its way into the Pacific, its first goal was to reach the island of Tahiti to carry out the expedition's objective of recording observations on the expected passage of Venus before the sun. The ship reached Tahiti in April 1769. As they approached, the crew had problems finding a place where they could anchor, and it appears that the indigenous Tahitians did not want them there, as people stood on the beaches holding and waving clubs as an apparent warning. On April 13, Cook found he could anchor the ship at a spot that would be called Matavai Bay. Once this was done, some of the indigenous people traveled out to the ship in canoes to greet the visitors. They threw fruit and coconuts onto the ship, and Cook and the crew offered beads as a gift in return.

The *Endeavour* was anchored in Matavai Bay in Tahiti for three months. During that time, some items from the ship were stolen by Tahitians, and two members of the crew deserted the ship and decided they wanted to stay on the island permanently. While in Tahiti, James Cook and Joseph Banks learned about the ancient practice of tattooing. It was Cook and Banks who first brought word of this practice to Great Britain. The artist on the *Endeavour*, Sydney Parkinson, drew images of the tattoos he saw, and Joseph Banks would eventually write about tattooing, describing the process he had witnessed.

On June 3, 1769, Cook and Banks observed the transit of Venus. They did their best in carrying out the assignment, but the rays of the sun rendered close observation impossible. This had been a problem in the past for other people who had tried to observe the phenomenon, causing general inaccuracy.

Some historians believe that James Cook had diplomatic skills advanced enough to make the indigenous population view him and his crew in a friendly light. Perhaps with the help of these skills, Cook and Banks managed to convince a Tahitian man called Omai to come back to England with them. When back in Britain, Banks brought Omai to different places in the country so that the people could see what a native Tahitian looked like and to add extra credibility to Banks' accounts. He even introduced Omai to the king. Omai would join Captain Cook's third voyage in 1776, so he could return to his home.

After the *Endeavour* had left Tahiti, the ship headed off in the direction of what would later be called New Zealand. New Zealand had not yet been properly discovered by any European, and it was believed that the land was part of the fabled southern continent today known as Antarctica.

The journey between Tahiti and New Zealand proved difficult. The crew had to deal with areas of incredibly strong winds called the "Roaring Forties" in order to reach New Zealand and make their way around the coast, charting the waters. The mission was dangerous, and there was a continual risk of being wrecked. It took more than six months for the charting of the coasts New Zealand's islands to be completed.

On this first visit to New Zealand, Cook put policies in place to help prevent potentially dangerous conflicts with the indigenous people, the Maori. He and his crew would make sure to show the power of their firearms first. Once they had done that, Cook instructed everyone to be fair and honest in their dealings with the Maori. He did not tolerate his men stealing from them, and would severely punish such actions.

Cook seems to have thought of the Maori as brave, artistic, and noble. He also believed them to be warlike. Additionally, he acknowledged that the presence of Europeans in New Zealand, and in the other places his crew explored, seemed to have negative effects on the native people. Their appearance exposed the indigenous population to new diseases to which they had no immunity, and it had a damaging effect on their behavior with regard to morals.

Cook's relatively respectful approach and manner towards indigenous people of the lands he discovered and visited was unusual at the time. Some historians believe that it was his humble background as well as his exposure to the Quaker discipline of the Walker family with whom he lived as a mariner apprentice that led to his ideas in this area. He seemed to have a much stronger appreciation for the value of human life and the possible merit of other cultures than other explorers at the time apparently possessed.

After their tasks in New Zealand had been accomplished, Cook and his crew made their way to the coast of what would one day be called Australia, making another historic discovery. It was on April 20, 1770, that the ship found itself on Australia's southeast coast. James Cook made sure to plant the British flag on land, to claim the east shore of the continent for King George. The entire crew spent a great deal of time collecting samples of plants and birds, as well as specimens from the giant gum trees. The indigenous people of Australia, however, were wary of the visitors and tried to stay away from them as much as possible. Australia's indigenous people had lived on that continent for more than 60,000 years. Their culture was—and is—the oldest still existing culture in the world.

A result of James Cook's discovery and claiming of Australia for Great Britain was that the British government eventually decided to make the territory a penal colony. The purpose of this was not only to send prisoners into exile but also to help solidify Britain's presence and claim to the land. Eighteen years after Cook's discovery, the first British convicts were transported to Australia.

Once Cook decided that the crew's time in Australia was over and they tried to set off, the ship found itself stuck in the Great Barrier Reef. The Great Barrier Reef is one of the world's most impressive natural formations, at more than 100 miles wide and 1,200 miles long. The *Endeavour* sustained a great deal of damage, but eventually, the crew was able to save the ship, and after much-needed reparations, they were able to continue the journey. The crew's experiences at the Great Barrier Reef were so harrowing that Cook took care to avoid approaching it on his future voyages.

The ship then traveled to Batavia, Indonesia, a port under Dutch control. Unfortunately, Batavia was horrendously unsanitary and riddled with disease. Cook and his crew became dangerously ill with malaria. While still in port at Batavia, seven of the sailors died. Even after they left and began making their way towards the Strait of Sunda through the Indian Ocean, men continued to die. So many were dreadfully ill that sometimes there were as few as twelve crew members able do the work necessary for the ship to sail. Despite the obstacles, Cook soon made his way to the Cape of Good Hope, known for its stormy winds and seas. The Cape of Good Hope is found in South Africa, at the Cape Peninsula's southern end. It was in 1488 that a Portuguese explorer first happened upon this spot, and it was there that Cook engaged an additional ten sailors to make up for their previous losses.

Through the leadership of Cook and the exertions of the crew, the ship made it back to England safely in 1771. The appearance of the ship in the English Channel caused quite a bit of surprise, as the *Endeavour* had been considered missing for a long period of time, and many people thought it had been lost.

The English newspapers were full of news of the expedition and its success. It must have been a frustration for Cook, however, to see that almost all publications named Banks as the leader, and even said that Banks was the man who discovered the new continent of Australia.

Despite Cook's accomplishments, Britain's class system still stood in the way of the promotions to which he was morally entitled. His official title was only lieutenant even though he was 43 years old. He was soon given a promotion, but only to the position of commander rather than captain.

While James Cook did not find the great southern continent that he was searching for, the voyage was considered to be a great success. One of the accomplishments that brought him the most acclaim was the accuracy and precision of the maps he created of remote and then mysterious places. It was his efforts in this regard that allowed Great Britain to obtain future access to Australia and New Zealand, thus changing the course of history.

Chapter Three

Cook's Second Voyage: The Resolution (1772-1775)

"From what I have said of the Natives of New-Holland they may appear to some to be the most wretched people upon Earth, but in reality they are far more happier than we Europeans; being wholly unacquainted not only with the superfluous but the necessary conveniences so much sought after in Europe, they are happy in not knowing the use of them."

—James Cook

Cook's respite in England was brief, but he was able to spend time with his family, which was a rare event. He had been gone for three years, and it can be imagined that he and his wife and children were pleased to see one another again. It can be assumed that Cook's family was quite enthralled to hear about his many adventures, and must have felt proud to have a person of such accomplishment closely connected to them.

It was the very next year, in 1772, that Cook set off for his second great voyage, this time on a ship called the H.M.S. *Resolution*. Finally, Cook had a ship—officially— under his command. It was accompanied by another vessel, called the H.M.S. *Adventure*, which was commanded by a Captain Furneaux.

Captain Furneaux was an experienced naval commander. He had served on the H.M.S. *Dolphin* under Samuel Wallis, which circumnavigated the globe between 1766 and 1768. On the *Adventure*, Captain Furneaux's first lieutenant was Joseph Shank, and his second lieutenant was Arthur Kempe. Captain Furneaux also had the assistance of James Tobias Swilley, his servant, as well as Lieutenant James Scott, who headed twelve marines and other members of the crew.

Joseph Banks, who was unfairly given so much of the credit for Cook's success on the first voyage, was originally meant to accompany Cook on this journey as well. Unluckily—or perhaps luckily—Joseph Banks refused to come in the end, as a special upper deck and other fittings that he felt were necessary for himself and his companions were not permitted to be built on the ship. Permission for this was denied because it would have made the ship top-heavy and put the officers and crew in unnecessary danger. After Banks had made his decision not to be included on the voyage, it was thought that the famous writer Samuel Johnson could be a replacement. Johnson, however, was not interested in the opportunity. In the end, two Royal Society scientists took Banks' place; a man called Johann Reinhold Forster and Georg Forster, his son.

With the crew members in place, the *Resolution* and the *Adventure* set off from Plymouth in England on June 13, 1772. This time the goal of finding the fabled great southern continent was overtly expressed. The European idea of a "great southern continent" was a land that would be full of riches and opportunity, equivalent to North America, not an inhospitable place of constant ice and snow, too cold for a human being to live. As we all know, Cook's thorough exploration found that no such new land of milk and honey existed. However, there is no way that anyone could claim that this voyage was unfruitful. James Cook's second voyage, like the first, was truly historic.

Cook continued in his dedication to ensuring the health and well-being of his crew through proper provisions. The two ships on this voyage brought along vast amounts of biscuits, olive oil, suet, sauerkraut (which helped to prevent scurvy), salt pork, salt beef, beer, pickled carrots (another anti-scurvy food), and, of course, water. The ships also had systems of water purification that had the capability of purifying contaminated fresh water and distilling salt water. Some of the other variety of items and supplies found on board were trinkets that could be used in bartering with native people, as well as necessary tools and hardware.

After the ships had left England, they traveled via Madeira, which they reached in July or August 1772, and Cape Town in South Africa, where they arrived a few months later. Subsequently, when the ships arrived at the Cape of Good Hope, the crew enjoyed a bit of a break. They continued soon after that, however, sailing to the southeast.

In January the following year, the *Resolution* and the *Discovery* became the first ships in the world ever known to break through the Antarctic Circle. Today, it's hard to imagine eighteenth-century explorers for the first time encountering the inhospitable cold and ice of Antarctica. One wonders if they realized the acute danger that confronted them. As Cook was a highly experienced seaman, he most certainly must have. His ambition, however, was almost limitless.

The large icebergs they encountered made it too dangerous to get as close as they would have liked to the mainland. Nonetheless, the discovery made James Cook the first commander to confirm the existence of Antarctica.

Antarctica is known for its blinding fogs, and the two ships even lost contact with one another at one point. Luckily, the sailors had foreseen that this might happen and had agreed on a place where they would meet up and continue the journey. The pre-arranged meeting point was in New Zealand, and both ships made their way to Queen Charlotte Sound separately, joining each other in June. Fortunately, this area had been charted by Cook a few years before. Queen Charlotte Sound is located on New Zealand's South Island, in its Marlborough region. The most eastern of the main sounds in the area, Queen Charlotte Sound is referred to by the native Maori as Totaranui.

After the two ships had reunited, they went on to the southern Pacific and visited Tahiti soon after. Afterward, they sailed to a place that Cook called the Friendly Islands, today known as the Republic of Tonga. The Republic of Tonga is in Polynesia and has 169 islands. Cook called these islands the Friendly Islands because he found the native people to be friendly and welcoming. In October, the *Resolution* and the *Adventure* were separated again, this time by a storm. Although both ships were safe, they were not able to meet up again until they returned to England at the end of the voyage.

After the separation, Cook decided to head back in the direction of Antarctica, as it was summer and he knew it would not be quite as inhospitable as it had been previously. He crossed the Antarctic Circle for the third time in January 1774. Once Cook had accomplished this final crossing of the Antarctic Circle, he headed north to do more exploration of the Pacific Ocean. He went to the Friendly Islands, Vanuatu, New Caledonia, Norfolk Island, and Easter Island during this journey.

Vanuatu is an archipelago in the Pacific with more than 80 islands, while New Caledonia is a French collection of islands about 900 miles east of Australia. The main island of New Caledonia is much larger than the rest. The smaller Norfolk Island was discovered by James Cook around 877 miles east of Australia. Cook was intrigued by the fact that there were giant pines and flax trees growing on the island which he knew would be useful for Britain, especially given the fact that the American Revolution had cut off an important source of lumber for England.

Easter Island, also in the South Pacific, is remotely located 2,500 miles east of Tahiti and 2,300 miles from the west coast of Chile. It was named Easter Island by the Dutch explorers who found it in 1722. When the

Resolution reached Easter Island, James Cook fell violently ill. He was unable to explore ashore, but he sent a party of his crew to do so in the island's southern region. The men marveled at the sight of the gigantic head statues which cover the area. An artist called William Hodges painted the stone statues to record what they looked like for the people back in England. Much later, in 1995, the Easter Island was named a UNESCO World Heritage Site for its cultural significance.

Other places that Cook visited on his second voyage include the Marquesas Islands, Raiatea, Vatoa, and the New Hebrides. The Marquesas Islands is a number of volcanic islands found in French Polynesia. Located in the same region, Raiatea is the second largest of a group of islands called the Society Islands. It is believed that Cook named them that in honor of the Royal Society in Britain.

Vatoa is the only island currently part of Fiji to which Cook ever ventured, while the New Hebrides was the name of a group of islands now known as Vanuatu. Located in the South Pacific, Vanuatu was discovered in 1606 by a Spanish explorer named Pedro Fernandes de Queirós, and it was only after Cook visited Vanuatu during this voyage in 1774 that the British and French colonized it. Cook did not receive a friendly reception by the indigenous New Hebrideans. The native people attempted to seize a boat, and Cook ordered that they be fired on as a result. In his journals, he said that he wanted to avoid deaths and tried to focus on the chief who had led the attack. Still, several people, as well as the chief, were killed, and there were injuries amongst both the native people and the ship's crew.

After this failure, Cook made his way towards what would eventually be known as the Cook Islands. Today, the islands are in a political association with New Zealand. The first Europeans to discover the Cook Islands were the Spanish in the sixteenth century. In 1595, Alvaro de Mendana de Neira, a Spanish sailor, recorded his sighting of the islands, but the first European to step foot on them was a Portuguese captain, Pedro Fernandes de Queirós, in 1606.

In 1773, Cook made his way to the island group. He called one of them Hervey Island, and this name was soon used to signify the southern Cook Islands. It was not until the 1820s that anyone referred to the islands as the Cook Islands in honor of James Cook.

Located west of the Cook Islands, Niue would be Cook's next stop. He was quite wary of this 100-square-mile island as no European ship had reached it before. When the *Resolution* first appeared in their waters, the inhabitants were evidently angry and refused to allow the crew ashore. Cook wrote of the experience that the native people of Niue were covered in a red substance that might have been blood, and on this basis, he referred to the place as "Savage Island." This name was used by Europeans for at least two centuries before the island's real name of Niue finally became widely known.

After these adventures, Cook returned to New Zealand's Queen Charlotte Sound. Later that year, he spent Christmas in South America, in a place that he would call Christmas Sound as a result. After that, Cook set out again and did further explorations of the South Atlantic. In doing so, he searched for a coastline that a famous geographer and hydrographer for the British Admiralty, Alexander Dalrymple, had predicted could exist. Cook, however, had to conclude that it did not.

After this, Cook sailed his ship to a place called Table Bay at the Cape Peninsula's northern end, a spot which was overlooked by Cape Town. It was there that the ship was refitted and made ready for the trip back to Britain. On the way home, Cook went to Fernando de Noronha, an island located off Brazil's northeast coast, and St. Helena. Finally, after being away for more than three years, Cook and his crew made it back to Portsmouth, England in July 1775.

Cook and the crew could now celebrate a well-executed mission. They had established not only the existence of Antarctica but also discovered archipelagos such as New Caledonia. Even though some were disappointed that the great southern continent as imagined by the British as a place of opportunity and potential wealth did not exist, James Cook was finally given the recognition that he had long deserved when the *Resolution* and the *Adventure* returned to England.

One of the most remarkable things about Cook's second journey was the fact that only four men died in the whole course of the expedition. This was very unusual in the eighteenth century, and it was due to Cook's strict rules concerning diet and hygiene for his men. He showed an awareness of the importance of cleanliness and the prevention of scurvy that was almost unique at this time in history.

During the journey, Cook had also brought a chronometer with him, which proved extremely useful. A chronometer is a special kind of timepiece that can help determine the longitude for more accurate navigation at sea. This was an entirely new technology at the time, and Cook had not had this instrument on his earlier voyage.

As a result of the success, Cook was awarded the rank of Captain by the Admiralty, given an honorary retirement (which he did not choose to make use of), received the appreciation of King George III, and became a fellow of the Royal Society. He was presented to the king and was awarded the Royal Society's Copley Medal for his achievements. He was also given the position of post-captain at Greenwich Hospital. Additionally, he created a written account of his voyage.

While Cook was given a chance the retire at this point, he did not want to cease with his expeditions. He was not satisfied yet and felt he still had more to discover.

Chapter Four

Cook's Third Voyage (1776-1779)

"Independent thinkers are usually geniuses or idiots and at times it's hard to tell which."

—James Cook

In 1775, James Cook started his work as post-captain at Greenwich Hospital. This was a job with a comfortable income and minimal duties; he was set for life without having to do very much else. There was no need for him to set off on another adventure.

But Cook seemed restless and wanted further achievements, and the Admiralty of the Royal Navy were keen on sending him on another expedition. They were acutely aware of his skills and believed that if anyone could find the Northwest Passage they were looking for, it would be him. The Royal Navy had no way of knowing, however, that Cook had changed inexplicably since his last journey and that this expedition was doomed to fail.

The Northwest Passage is a passage of water at the top of North America in the Arctic that connects the Atlantic and Pacific Oceans. Europeans were eager to find it, as it would mean that mariners would be able to travel to the

Pacific and Eastern regions of the globe (such as China) without undergoing the long and treacherous journey around the southern tip of Africa. If the Northwest Passage existed, it would mean that the route to China and India would be much shorter and quicker. One of the many reasons that this was important at the time was the British love of tea, a commodity grown in the East.

Still, the Northwest Passage was a matter of contention. Some people doubted that it even existed, and it had certainly never been found or successfully passed through. Therefore, the Admiralty were eager to send Cook on a voyage to search for—and hopefully pass through—the passage. Cook also had an additional incentive to sail; Omai, the Tahitian that he and Banks had brought to England, wanted to return home to Tahiti.

In 1776, Cook was preparing to sail the *Resolution* once again. The ship had been repaired, but unfortunately, Cook did not make himself present at the shipyard where the restoration was carried out. He had always supervised such activities in the past, and that had been a key factor in the safety and success of his expeditions. It is believed that this lapse was due to Cook being busy writing about his second voyage.

Just like during that second journey, the *Resolution* was not to sail alone. It would be accompanied by Cook's smallest ship, a vessel called the *Discovery*. At the king's request, both the *Resolution* and the *Discovery* carried a substantial amount of livestock. The animals were likely meant for future settlers in New Zealand. This is believed to have annoyed Cook and created complications in the journey.

Before the third voyage began officially, the *Resolution* made its way via the Canary Islands to South Africa's Cape Town to join with the *Discovery*. Then, with James Cook commanding the *Resolution,* and Charles Clerke behind the wheel of the *Discovery*, the two ships set off together for New Zealand in December 1776.

As his first mission, Cook sailed the *Resolution* across the South Indian Ocean and was able to confirm the location of Desolation Island. At this island, later renamed Kerguelen Island, Cook and his crew found large numbers of penguins and seals. The crew killed a great many of them and used their oil to fuel their lamps amongst other things. Cook called this area Christmas Harbor, as Christmas was just about to begin.

After this, Cook sailed eastward. In January 1777, he arrived in Tasmania (also known at that time as Van Diemen's Land), and in February he reached New Zealand's Queen Charlotte Sound. Cook was well acquainted with the area from his previous journeys, and three years earlier, a Maori leader had killed one of his crew members. Because of this, the native people seemed afraid that the British were returning for revenge. Cook, however, did not have vengeance on his mind. He made a point of befriending the Maori man who had led the attack against the *Adventure*, helping to ensure a peaceful atmosphere.

The *Resolution* and the *Discovery* remained in New Zealand for almost two weeks. During that time, the crew traded with the Maori in Ship Cove and successfully restocked the ship with wild celery and a special grass that Cook called "scurvy grass." Cook never forgot the critical importance of having fresh vegetables and fruits onboard as a part of his crew's diet, to help prevent scurvy.

After the short reprieve, Cook sailed to the islands of the South Pacific from February 1777 and spent time in the Cook Islands in April. In July, his ship went to the Tongan Islands, and from August to December, it was in Tahiti. Omai, the Tahitian, was finally home again.

During this part of the journey, Cook discovered Hawaii. He called the group of islands the Sandwich Islands, naming them after one of his superiors. After the discovery, Cook set sail to the northeast with the intention of exploring North America's west coast, specifically the part of the coast that was north of the Spanish settlements in Alta, California. On March 6, Cook landed in today's Oregon, naming this area Cape Foulweather.

The crew soon began moving northwards up the coast. Cook eventually entered Nootka Sound situated on Vancouver Island, after passing the Strait of Juan de Fuca without realizing it. Cook decided to anchor near Yuquot, a First Nations village. While there was some tension between the native people of Yuquot and the crew, there was a measure of friendly interaction.

Cook found that the native people of this area of North America were a bit savvier in trading than some others, demanding items of greater value in exchange for what they gave. The natives asked for relatively expensive things such as metal objects, but they could also offer valuable items such as sea otter pelts in return.

After leaving this area, Cook mapped the coast from this point moving north towards the Bering Strait, eventually completing the notable accomplishment of charting most of the northwest coastline of North America.

During the northward journey, the *Resolution* came upon the area that would one day be called Cook Inlet in Alaska. From there, the crew made its way to the Bering Strait. When arriving, however, Cook became frustrated as he found the channel impassable. Acting increasingly irrational and sometimes aggressive, the captain made several attempts to cross the strait but had to find himself defeated in the end. This new side to Cook's personality, however, would not revert so easily.

To the crew, Cook's behavior became almost or entirely unrecognizable. He became overwhelmingly angry at times, alarming his men with outbursts of temper. At one point, he tried to force his crew to eat walrus meat that they found to be disgusting. He also showed a measure of cruelty that was considered altogether out of character by everyone on the ship. While his punishments for transgressions committed by the crew and indigenous peoples in the past had been measured and moderate, he now ordered villages to be burned and for individuals' ears to be cut off. It can easily be imagined how terrified the people under Cook's command and the native people he came across were to deal with this seemingly new, cruel captain. Conditions became so bad on this third great expedition that the crew wrote a letter to Cook setting out their complaints. This was an extremely rare step for a crew to take in the eighteenth century, as the utmost deference to one's superiors was drilled into the heads of Royal Navy members. Unfortunately, being tormented by an unknown stomach condition seemed to contribute to Cook's change in temperament, and the outlook for improvement proved continuously dark.

Plagued by these difficulties, the crew set off for another visit to Hawaii in October 1778. The *Resolution* and the *Discovery* arrived one month later and then continued to sail around the Hawaiian Islands for about two months, seeking for a suitable place to anchor. The two ships finally found a place to land in the middle of January 1779.

Native Hawaiians in canoes accompanied the ships as they made their way around, offering generous presents and even coming aboard to extend their gratuities. Cook did not realize, but it was currently a sacred festival for the native people. The Hawaiians interpreted the arrival of the two ships to be spiritually significant. Cook must have been surprised when some of the indigenous people appeared to worship him; they believed that he might be an incarnation of a deity, Lono.

During this stay at the Hawaiian Islands, the men enjoyed the friendly atmosphere with the indigenous people of Hawaii. There was energetic trading for all sorts of goods, and Cook and his crew even had sociable celebrations with the native people. But eventually, Cook sensed that he and his men might have overstayed their welcome, putting a strain on the native people's way of life and stock of supplies. As he had accomplished what he needed at that time, he decided it was time to leave, and the ship set off on February 4, 1779.

Unfortunately, after they set sail, the *Resolution* was battered by serious storms. A result of shoddy workmanship, a mast of the ship was broken, something that would not have happened if Cook had supervised the work and repairs that had taken place before the voyage. The *Resolution* had no choice but to return to the Hawaiian Islands to do repairs on February 11.

For a number of different reasons, the indigenous Hawaiians were not pleased to see Cook and his crew again, and it was reported that some of the native people stole the *Discovery*'s cutter. To try to ensure the return of the cutter, Cook made the inadvisable decision to hold the Hawaiian king hostage until the cutter was returned. That decision would cost Cook his life.

On February 14, 1779, James Cook was killed by the indigenous people in a violent altercation, and his body was taken into a forest area. It is believed that he may have been partially eaten, but there is no conclusive proof of such an occurrence. Another possibility is that the respect that the native people had for Cook resulted in him being given a funerary ritual typically used for the most important people in this indigenous society. It does seem that rituals such as disemboweling and removal of flesh from the bones were done.

The native people brought some of Cook's flesh to his remaining crew and Charles Clerke, the captain of the *Discovery*. The action might have been meant as an overture of peace. The crew and Clerke decided to bury this flesh at sea.

Cook's death was a dreadful blow to Clerke and the men of both ships. Clerke tried to continue to the expedition, and he set off for the remaining islands of Hawaii. After that, he sailed northwards to look for the Northwest Passage. At this point, Clerke contracted tuberculosis, and he died as a result in August 1779, after trying yet again to pass the Bering Strait.

A man named John Gore was put in charge of the expedition, and the ships went on to Macao in China after sailing by Japan's coast. After that, they traveled via Cape Town and returned to Britain in 1780.

We can only imagine how devastated Cook's wife, Elizabeth, and their surviving children must have been once notified of James' death. Only three children were still alive when James Cook was killed; James, Nathaniel, and Hugh. At that point, the one who would prove the longest lived of all, James, was 16. He would reach the age of 31. Hugh Cook was only three years old when his father was killed. He would live until 1793 and the age of 17. At the time of his father's death, Nathaniel was 15, and he would die in 1780, just one year later.

The eldest son, James, joined the Royal Navy as a young man, possibly hoping for a glorious career like his father's. He would go on to command a ship called H.M.S. *Spitfire* for a very brief period. In 1794, James died as result of drowning. His mother, Elizabeth Cook, lived into her 90s (an unusual accomplishment in the eighteenth century), passing in 1835, 56 years after her husband.

Both of Captain James Cook's sisters, Christiana and Margaret, survived his death. Their father lived until April 1779, just months after his son was killed. He enjoyed a long life, reaching the age of 85. Cook's mother, Grace, died earlier on in 1765. After Grace's death, the elder James Cook had gone to live with one of his daughters.

Chapter Five

The Legacy of James Cook

"If you would not be forgotten as soon as you are dead, either write something worth reading or do something worth writing."

—Benjamin Franklin

No one could ever question the profound impact that James Cook and his voyages have had on the modern world. The world that we live in right now would have been very different if James Cook had never lived. Some might say it would even be unrecognizable in many respects.

James Cook is considered by many to be the greatest explorer that ever lived. Not only was he a courageous and ambitious mariner and leader of men, but he was also humble enough to learn the scientific skills needed to achieve an unprecedented level of accuracy in his charting and cartography, as well as his marine surveying, which included inspecting ships and supervising their repair.

James Cook was an innovative thinker who was unafraid of trying new things that he believed would work. Examples include the unique care he took with regard to his crews' health and well-being. While all mariners knew about the horrible disease of scurvy, no one had taken the time to come up with a system for its prevention. Cook's scurvy-free ships and low illness and death rates in his crews made him revolutionary in this respect.

James Cook showed that it was best to take a rational and measured approach to exploration. Before him, commanders and captains tended to see expeditions purely as a means to their desire for glory, viewing scientific methods almost with disdain. Crews were seen as expendable, and indigenous people in the places discovered and explored were often treated in a confrontational and adversarial manner. Cook showed that adopting a more humble, introspective, and respectful manner was a much better option.

It was James Cook's discovery of Australia and New Zealand and his action of claiming these lands for the British Crown that made the current nature of the British Empire possible. While this was a significant achievement for which Cook will always be remembered positively by some people, others—such as the indigenous people of Australia, New Zealand, and other places where Cook landed—cannot help but see him in a negative light. For them, Cook and his expeditions were a destructive force leading to trauma for the natives and changing their world for all generations to come. The bad behavior that Cook exhibited on his last, disastrous expedition contributes to these feelings.

James Cook was a complex figure with both good and bad characteristics. Regardless of one's take on him and his voyages, there can be no doubt of his extraordinary impact on the world.

Conclusion

Today, James Cook is a household name. Few in the Western world have never heard of him, and it's difficult to find a person who does not know that he was a great mariner and explorer.

While he is both loved and hated, no one can deny Cook's immortal fame. We have learned that James Cook was an extraordinarily talented and intelligent man, but also that, like many other human beings, he was dreadfully flawed.

For all of Cook's many faults, most of us can acknowledge that the captain's determination and sense of vision for what he could accomplish was something worth respecting. The question of whether his efforts were given the right direction is one that is up for greater debate.

When we think of James Cook, it is vital to think of him in his historical context. He was a bright boy born into a family of farm laborers in a discouragingly stratified and unfair society. With his limited education, options were extremely few. He saw that the Royal Navy might be the place for him, because of its relative abundance of opportunity and his enthusiasm for the sea and adventure.

The young Cook felt the need to prove himself and show his abilities to the world, and he succeeded in doing so for the course of his life. There can be little doubt that James Cook made his family and everyone associated with him proud as he traveled around the globe and accomplished things that would have been unthinkable in earlier times, especially for the son of a laborer.

49309294R00027

Made in the USA
Middletown, DE
13 October 2017